John Henri Moser

Painting Utah Modern

John Henri Moser
Painting Utah Modern

Kenneth Hartvigsen, Mark Callister, and Sharron Brim

BRIGHAM YOUNG UNIVERSITY
MUSEUM OF ART

Published on the occasion of the exhibition *John Henri Moser: Painting Utah Modern*. Brigham Young University Museum of Art, February 28 to October 10, 2020.

This book and the exhibition it acompanies are made possible through the generosity of Sharron Brim, Mark Callister, and Brigham Young University.

Library of Congress Control Number: 2020917737

Catalog design by Jeffrey R. Barney

Cover: Plate 28, *Pink Mountain*, no date. Oil on canvas board, 11 X 21½ inches. Sharron Brim collection, detail.

Frontispiece: Plate 11, *Red Butte River*, no date. Oil, 22 x 16 inches. Courtesy of Church History Museum, detail.

Table of Contents

John Henri Moser: Painting Utah Modern

By Kenneth Hartvigsen, PhD

To those who love Utah art, the name John Henri Moser conjures images of vibrant landscapes, dynamic color combinations, and thick, loose brushstrokes. Moser's style, rich in pigment, expressive and playful as it traverses the boundary between objective reality and personal experience, has always found appeal among private collectors as well as collecting institutions; every major museum in the State of Utah has Mosers in its vaults. So, why have there not been more Moser exhibitions, and what does it mean to be showing his work now? His paintings have certainly been seen, but *John Henri Moser: Painting Utah Modern* at the BYU Museum of Art is Moser's first solo museum show. Considering that he died in 1951 and that he was not "re-discovered" but has been hiding in plain sight in significant gallery and museum collections, this oversight seems almost unforgivable. Answering the why, requires untangling the interwoven inquiries of who and what. Who was John Henri Moser, and what was he doing, painting expressionistic landscapes in the conservative artistic world of early twentieth-century Utah? What can his work say to contemporary audiences?

John Henri Moser explored the Utah landscape with painterly abandon at a time when his local art world was generally more reserved. Moser's granddaughter, Sharron Brim, who participated in this exhibition and catalog, remembers her grandfather defending is vibrant color choices to artistic friends He objected to their complaints, which I'm sure he did often throughout his career, when he presented landscapes with flame orange trees, violet skies, and pink mountains. That his artist friends did not always understand his aesthetic choices is one small bit of evidence in the

Opposite:
Murray Canyon from Wellsville Dam (Wellsville Mountain)
1930, oil on board, 19 x 23 inches
Susan and Mark Callister
Collection, detail.

case for why Moser has not featured as prominently as he deserves. Looking closely at his life and career provides plenty of reasons that now is the time to take him more seriously.

Born in Switzerland in 1876, Moser emigrated to Utah with his family at age 12, after converting to The Church of Jesus Christ of Latter-Day Saints. An industrious youth, he worked on farms, in mines, and in a print shop, to earn money for college. He entered Utah State Agricultural College (now Utah State University) to study enginerring. He changed the course of studies thanks to a lifelong interest in art and the mentorship of teachers who recognized his artistic talent. With a loan from University president John A. Widtsoe, in exchange for Moser's promise to return and teach at the college, the fledgling artist traveled to Paris in 1908 to study academic painting.

The early twentieth century was a marvelous time to be an artist in Paris, as European art swirled with possibilities. The art academies continued their reign over historical tradition, and that is what Moser was seeking. Academic training emphasized anatomical study, draghtsmanship, and the use of established compositional techniques, to prepare the most gifted students to produce grand history paintings and elegant portraits. While this educational model had served well for centuries, by the late nineteenth century a riotous artistic chorus called out for new techniques and styles that would engage with the ever-evolving realities of modern life. By the time Moser arrived in Paris, modernism in many guises was charging full-speed ahead on a track parallel, if not perpendicular to, the Academy's trajectory. Beginning with the Realists such as Gustave Courbet (1819–1877), modernists of various stripes had gained ground. Although Moser had come to Paris to study in the academic mode, he was in for a much broader education.

Arriving in Paris nearly half a century after modernism's earliest adventures, Moser would have encountered controversial techniques of the past, now being assimilated into the evolving sphere of accepted art practice. Realists and Impressionists who had caused scandal in the Paris Salons of the 1850s, 60s, and 70s, were now old guard rather than avant-garde. Post-Impressionists, such as Paul Cézanne (1839–1906) and Vincent van Gogh (1853–1890) were entering a new phase of postmortem lionization.

Cézanne, who died in 1906, received the honor of a major retrospective at the Autumn Salon in 1907, just one year before Moser's arrival. Cézanne's geometric abstraction in traditional genres, his flattened landscapes of patterned shapes and still-life paintings with multiple simultaneous points of view, were no longer the curious experiments of a single artist detached from Paris's gravitational pull—they were a celebrated inspiration for new waves of artistic invention. Moser might have seen this influence in Cubism's embryonic form, which was still developing in Georges Braque and Pablo Picasso's studios. Though their styles never converged, Moser knew Picasso, and may have been an early witness to Cubism's challenging distortions.

Van Gogh's influence was no less palpable than Cézanne's at the turn of the century, as many artists sought new modes of emotional expression in color and form. Though he was a poor student in Paris, Moser may have been aware of the Expressionists working in Germany, as artists such as Kirchner and Marc were shocking viewers with violent color combinations, angular and often cramped compositions, and distorted figures that communicated emotional and psychological states rather than visual reality. While Moser may never have seen Expressionist exhibitions in Dresden or Berlin, art ably travels across international borders, and there were ample opportunities to see daring and exuberant colorism in Paris.[1]

By 1908, France's most notorious colorists, known as the *Fauves* (meaning "wild beasts") were no longer working or exhibiting as a unified group. Despite the movement's short lifespan, its influence and legacy were firmly in place. Expanding on Post-Impressionism's color theory (exemplified in Van Gogh and Gaugin's highly saturated hues) and realistic yet non-imitative rendering of the natural world (as seen in Van Gogh's stylized brushstroke and Cezanne's geometric invention), Henri Matisse (1869–1954), André Derain (1880–1954), and others freed color from the necessity of replicating objective reality. For the Fauves, bold application of color served as a powerful tool of emotional expression, and at times was potent enough to be the painting's chief goal.

While color was not their only innovation, it certainly defined their moment of glory. In December 1908, when Moser was already in Paris, Matisse published "Notes of an Artist," in the Parisian Journal *La Grande Revue*. In this essay, his first attempt to theorize his artistic process, Matisse articulated his belief in color's expressive qualities.[2]

> "I cannot copy nature in a servile way; I am forced to interpret nature and submit it to the spirit of the picture. From the relationship I have found in all the tones, there must result a living harmony of colors, a harmony analogous to that of a musical composition…The chief function of color should be to serve expression as well as possible."[3]

Matisse was uninterested in "copying," nature, and sought rather to unlock new expressive possibilities by combining colors and celebrating their interrelated visual harmonies. The artist further clarified that in his work color could be arbitrary and still invoke powerful effects: "I put down my tones without a preconceived plan… My choice of colors does not rest on any scientific theory; it is based on observation, on sensitivity, on felt experiences."[4] While Matisse does say that his colors are based on observation, he is clear that this observation need not be purely visual. His colors may indeed come from his experience, but they may also come from non-visual sensitivity.

John Henri Moser was a sensitive man, stirred by love, faith, and beauty. It is no surprise that the emotionally and visually expressive paintings of the Fauves left a mark on his soul. However, there is little in his own Parisian work to hint at this profound influence. Even though Moser was in Paris at just the right time to see early modernism swirling through the air in kaleidoscopic color, he was there for academic structure, to build an enduring foundation in traditional drawing and composition. Picasso was creating his most challenging work to date during the time that he and Moser were acquainted, but this did not drive Moser to an artistic frenzy. While it remains uncertain whether Moser and Matisse ever met (Mark Callister's essay in this volume provides a compelling argument that such a meeting was not only possible, but likely), the Fauve's gravitational pull in Moser's circle is clear. During the time that Moser was in Paris, Matisse was pushing modernism even further than he had in his earlier Fauvist works as he explored the possibilities of extreme color and geometric simplicity in a flattened, non-illusionistic pictorial space. But Moser, enamored with the French landscape that he explored in his free time, painted river scenes and stands of trees that recalled the Barbizon painters of the 19th century, such as Jean-Baptiste-Camille Corot (1796–1875) and Charles-François Daubigny (1817–1878). Something in the landscape held him transfixed, and provided a foundation for what would become his life's work.

During this formative period, Moser wrote to his wife that his greatest desire was not to achieve fame or accumulate wealth, but rather to share the gospel of Jesus Christ through his art. As a devout member of The Church of Jesus Christ of Latter-Day Saints, and a budding artist, he would have known about the "art missionaries," who were called by Church leadership to study in Paris in order to bring more artistic sophistication to the Church's architectural and artistic projects. The Paris Art Mission, however was a not a recurring Church program, and those artists began their studies nearly two decades before Moser's own journey. Still, Moser believed he had been called to testify of God's love by celebrating the beauty of all creation, and he saw his time in Paris as a fulfillment of that calling. In one letter to his wife Aldine, he explained:

> My intension (sic) is to serve God and beautify his holy cause of bringing to light some
> of the beautiful nature that he has given us, not just for the money but for the joy that I
> receive while in this life. Such is my work. Some may call me fool, but we shall see upon the
> other shore whose jugment (sic) was the best.[5]

Despite the relative conservatism of his Parisian paintings, there is evidence that Moser, at least on occasion, foresaw that his time in Paris would prepare him to share his faith through unexpected and even challenging means.

"When I come home people will not understand my work…" Moser warned his wife in a letter dated September 1909. "It takes years for people to open their eyes and look."[6] Such a pointed, even proud pronouncement seems unexpected when viewing paintings such as *French Landscape Near Paris* (plate 3) and *Countryside Paris* (plate 4), two charming examples of his French period. The former revels in atmosphere, inviting the viewer into a secluded and quiet experience, while the latter's light and airy ambiance transforms a row of reaching trees into a joyous embodiment of environmental energies, as though this small piece of land is waking up and stretching toward the sky. But, would Moser, surrounded by modernism's boundless artistic possibilities, think that work like this would prove too challenging for his Utah audience? Perhaps. This same letter references Alma B. Wright, an art professor at Brigham Young College and the University of Utah, who according to Moser was, "suffering from the critics…"[7] Wright and Moser were in communication, and it is possible that Wright, by way of friendly warning, was preparing the younger artist for the difficult path of a career in the arts. Another more romantic, although unverifiable possibility is that in a moment of intro-spection Moser wondered about his own artistic future. "There is no rest for the artist so long as his eyes are open," he had written to Aldine only two weeks earlier, "and when they are closed the mind is at thought."[8] Though he loved painting in nature, Moser knew that the artist's work included contemplation. Surrounded on all sides by artistic possibility yet studying academic tradition, did Henri wonder which path he would take?

Moser returned to Utah in 1910, and once again enjoyed the spiritual and emotional support of his loving wife and children. He reconnected with the people and places he loved most. In fulfillment of his promise to John A. Widstoe, he began teaching, first in Logan, and then at the Branch Agricultural College in Cedar City, Utah. It was there, at home, that Moser's personal artistic style began to emerge—not in Paris, not in an academic atelier or an avant-garde gallery. *Peaceful Evening* (plate 7), painted five years after Moser's return, reveals his continuing evolution. While the subject has not changed much from his student days, his style and technique rely more on Fauvism and Post-Impres-sionism than on academic standards. Vibrant colors peek out of the shadows and dance across the grasses and brush of the foreground; tree trunks, dappled with colorful light, spring into fiery foliage created not with elegant linear detail, but with bold, confident patches. *Green Aspens, Blue Background* (plate 32), is more audacious in its technique. Snaking tendril-trees rise from a patchwork field of yellow, green, and blue spots—a rhythmic texture of dots and dashes. Unwavering in his love of leafy scenery, Moser offers here not a quiet sojourn in a Barbizon forest, but a Fauvist celebration of color. These trees don't sway in the breeze—uninhibited they dance, as lively and emboldened as Matisse's famous figures holding hands in their joyous circle.

Moser's mature work draws from many types of views, yet a survey of his Oeuvre reveals an affection for certain locations: Bear Lake, Jenny Lake, the Tetons. Like Claude Monet and Paul Cezanne, two artists whose influence was still reverberating through Paris during his studies, Moser loved returning to familiar scenes, and seemed to experience them each time as if they were new to him. Sharron Brim recalls her grandfather marveling aloud at nature's beauty, even when he was surrounded by mountains, lakes, and canyons he had seen virtually his whole life. Like Cezanne, whose repeated visits to Mont Sainte-Victoire reveal the artist's personal evolution, Moser's act of returning to the familiar freed him to explore color and shape in sometimes startling ways. In *Tetons from Jenny Lake* (plate 30) Moser's mountains are a row of craggy teeth chewing along the horizon, their peaks, and slides form flat planes of aubergine, pink, and slate. Trees, almost human-like, bunch in the foreground, keeping their long vigil of the monstrous rocky forms across the lake. With a command of color and a mind freed from the necessity of replicating nature, Moser, like Matisse, refuses to merely describe what he sees, choosing instead to paint what he feels, what he knows to be true.

As Moser expressed again and again in his letters home from Paris, his purpose in painting was to preach, to testify of the joy and beauty of God's creation. Thus, his art cannot be appreciated fully without considering his abiding spirituality. Looking at *Red Stone Canyon, Zion* (plate 14) or *Quaking Aspens, Old Homestead* (plate 38) leaves little doubt about what artistic experiences had pricked Moser the most deeply in Paris. His love of geometric simplification, the rhythmic repetition of confident and wide brushstrokes, and above all his consistent coloristic expressiveness, testify that he found much to admire in the modernists. Yet Moser's enduring religious devotion set him apart from much of the avant-garde. For him, modern art's exhilarating palette was not in itself an artistic end, nor was it an intellectual game or mode of visual experimentation. Moser's modernism was an instrument of faith, a tool for expressing his love of God and the glory of all creation.

When Moser died in 1951, he left behind a body of work that, despite immediate appearances, defies simple explanation. In a state celebrated for its dramatic vistas, he is one of many artists who focused on Utah's landscape. He did so, however, with a flair for unexpected color combinations, and a desire to infuse personal meaning into his essentialized views. These modernist leanings set him apart from many Utah painters. Yet, his spiritual vision and desire to testify through his art separate him from the avant-garde, as does a career spent largely in an artistically conservative environment. Not daring enough and too religious for the modernists, too loose and bold for the conservative crowd, John Henri Moser remained an artist apart, dedicated until the end of his life to his personal artistic vision.

John Henri Moser's artistic legacy has suffered, in part, from the fact that while he is represented in museum collections, many of his best works remain in private hands. This exhibition, borrowing from private collectors as well as from every major art museum in the state of Utah, seeks to provide a view of the artist's progression by exhibiting his greatest masterworks together for the very first time. It also argues that Moser's time has finally come, not by placing him neatly in any one box, but by allowing him room to define his own artistic orthodoxy. I would argue that Moser was a true modernist, in that he studied and thought deeply, and made purposeful artistic decisions based on what traditions and techniques did and did not allow him to express his experience of reality. Moser's greatness need not be defined by how well he fits into any one narrative, for example whether or not his work represents the narrative of Fauvism, or of Utah, of western landscape tradition, or his faith. Rather, contemporary audiences are prepared to learn from Moser's multiplicity and imperfections, by the ways in which the elements of his life weave together and create a compelling picture of an artist who learned from the past and absorbed the present, who looked to this world in hopes of receiving visions of heaven.

Dr. Kenneth Hartvigsen is the curator of American Art at the Brigham Young University Museum of Art in Provo Utah. He holds a doctorate in art history from Boston University where he studied American Art and visual culture. In addition to his curatorial work, he has taught art history courses at Boston University, Weber State University, Westminster College, and BYU. Kenneth lives in Murray, Utah with his wife and two daughters.

End Notes

1. While Expressionism is often portrayed as a German movement, a more nuanced view recognizes its international cosmopolitan character. See Timothy O. Benson, *Expressionism in Germany and France from Matisse to the Blue Rider* (Zurich: Kunsthaus Zürich; Neue Galerie, 2014); Annegret Hoberg, Isabelle Jansen, Olaf Peters, et al., *Franz Marc and August Macke 1909-1914* (London, New York: Prestel, 2018).

2. Jack D. Flam, *Matisse on Art* (New York: E.P. Dutton, 1978), 32.

3. Henri Matisse, "Notes of an Artist," translation in Flam, 37–38. I have taken the liberty of substituting "color," for Flam's original use of the English "colour."

4. Ibid.

5. John Henri Moser, Letter to Aldine Moser, 21 February 1909, quoted in Thomas Moyle Alder, *Pathway to Color: The Art and Life of Henri Moser*, Masters Thesis, University of Utah, 2007, 42.

6. Moser, 12 September 1909, quoted in Alder, 37.
7. Ibif.

8. Moser, 3 September 1909, quoted in Alder, 37.

Battling for Place:
The Legacy of John Henri Moser

By Mark Callister

In paying tribute to Utah artist John Henri Moser who died in 1951, John A. Widtsoe, an apostle in the Church of Jesus Christ of Latter-Day Saints, described him as a man who "dreamed dreams and saw visions which appeared in time on his canvases [and who] lived in a great world, such as most of us are not able to enter." The Apostle acknowledged that the "world does not deal too kindly" with such visionaries and that Henri "had to battle for his rights and place among those who give gifts to the world." But he assured Henri's wife Aldine that Moser would "live on in the memory of the people. His paintings will become more and more sought after as the years go on. The power of his symbolism in color and design will be as a legacy to his generation."[1]

That legacy is tied to Fauvism —a revolutionary art movement that captured Moser's attention when he was studying academic painting in France. Having burst onto the Paris art scene in 1905, Fauvism was just ending when Henri Moser arrived in December 1908. The movement's most significant characteristic, however, its focus on freeing color from being used as a mere tool of representation, had left its mark. Inspired by Vincent van Gogh (1853–1890), Paul Gauguin (1848–1903), Georges Seurat (1859–1891) and Paul Cezanne (1839–1906), Fauvists broke with traditional representational style by using erratic, forceful brushstrokes, bold simplified shapes, and an emotional color theory that was meant to please and instill a sense of well-being, rather than to replicate the visual experience of everyday life.

Henri Matisse (1869–1954) was the unofficial leader of the group, which also included Albert Marquet (1875–1947), Charles Manguin (1874–1949), Charles Camoin (1879–1965), Jules Flandrin and others

Opposite:
Sardine Canyon
No date, oil on board,
19 x 23 inches
Susan and Mark Callister
Collection, detail.

who had studied under Symbolist painter Gustave Moreau (1826–1898), at the École des Beaux-Arts in Paris. Moreau pushed his students to think outside the lines of a formal aesthetic and to follow their own vision. Following Moreau's death Matisse and Marquet studied under Eugène Carrière (1849–1906) where they met Andre Derain (1880–1954), Jean Puy (1876–1960), and Pierre Laprade (1875–1931). Other artists who went through a Fauvist period include Georges Braque (1882–1963), Picasso's partner in Cubism, the Dutch painter Kees van Dongen (1877–1968), Raoul Dufy(1877–1953), Othon Friesz (1879–1949) and Louis Valtat (1869–1952).[2]

Fauvism's greatest contributions to modern art was its radical separation of color from its descriptive, representational purpose. Color could project a mood and establish a structure within the work of art without having to represent the natural world. The Fauves' simplified forms and saturated colors drew attention to the inherent flatness of the canvas, which in turn challenged academic painting's illusionistic perspective. Above all, Fauvism valued individual expression. The artist's experience of the subject, emotional response to nature, and intuition were all more important than academic theory or elevated subject matter.[3]

Although Fauvism as a movement lasted only from 1904 to 1908, the group's artistic output had tremendous impact. The greatest influence may have been felt in Germany where German Expressionists used violent colors without any concern for realism. Some American artists, however, also witnessed the ascendancy of the Fauves, and the innovative styles of Arthur Dove (1880–1946), John Marin (1870–1953), and Marsden Hartley (1877–1943), owe much to the Fauvist revolution. As this essay argues, John Henri Moser, an artist who spent most of his career painting the Utah landscape, should likewise be remembered for his expressive palette and bold loosening of form, as he was one of the first to bring European modernist style to Utah.

John Henri Moser was born in Wabern, Switzerland on September 13, 1876. His father Johann Moser was a stone cutter. The fifth of seven children, Henri, his mother and his brother Ernst converted to The Church of Jesus Christ of Latter-Day Saints in 1888, and Ernest and Henri emigrated to America the same year. Henri lived with the Diem family in Payson and spent ten years working both on their farm and for a printing establishment in Enterprise, Utah. In 1898 he took a job in Montana at the Gilt Edge mine to earn money for his education at the Utah State Agricultural College (now Utah State University) in Logan. On September 13, 1905 he married Aldine Wursten. The following year he left USAC to attend Brigham Young College in Logan and studied under Utah artist A.B. Wright from 1906 –08. Receiving encouragement and a loan from his friend, Dr. John A. Widtsoe, President of USAC, Moser agreed to study art in Paris in exchange for a commitment to teach at the school when he returned. Moser left for Paris in December 1908 traveling through Chicago where he visited the Art Institute of Chicago. On December 12, 1908, he boarded a ship in Portland Maine bound for Liverpool England.[4]

After arriving in Paris Moser enrolled at the Colarossi Night School[5], and the Académie Delécluse[6] where he studied with Marcel Berenaux. In addition, he studied with Jean-Paul Laurens (1838–1921) and Lucien Simon (1861–1945),[7] and became a member of the American Art Association of Paris (AAAP). The year before Moser arrived in Paris, the Association held an exhibition of American modernist art that marked a departure from its previous preference for academic styles. The January 1908 exhibition challenged the authority of another American artists' association, the Paris Society of American Painters (PSAP), which was more conservative in its insistence on academic styles. The 1908 exhibition at the AAAP represented a new generation of "younger" artists challenging their elders with works that emphasized artistic individuality and showed new forms of expression.[8] His decision to affiliate with the younger suggests that Moser remained open to revolutionary ideas that contrasted with the conservative academic style that he was sent to learn in Paris. In letters home Moser frequently declared his purpose for pursuing art, which was to serve God by celebrating His glorious gift of the natural world.

His confidence in this artistic path sustained him in humble circumstances, exemplified by the living quarters he had secured at No. P Passage du Lac, 15eme arrondissement, which he described as "10 feet by 12 feet with a bed, table and chair."[10] Rather than wearing him down, this austerity seems to have sharpened his resolve as Moser later wrote, "Now I am happy because I feel that really I am called to become an artist by God. It is by his hand that I am here to learn of the great world and to return and work for his great cause: the gospel."

In November 1909 Moser informed Aldine that he was starting at another school, the Miller & Carrie Academy to study portraiture painting.[11] There Moser met Frank Ignatius Serafic Zimbeaux, a neo-romantic tonalist painter originally from Pittsburgh, Pennsylvania. Zimbeaux has been described as a friend of Matisse, raising the possibility that Moser was introduced to Fauvism, and perhaps to Matisse himself, through Zimbeaux.[12] Although no evidence of a meeting between Moser and Matisse is known, the details of Moser's study in Paris from December 1908 to June 1910 demonstrate that the two artists circulated in some of the same social and artistic spaces, making the possibility of such an association all the more tantalizing.

Moser lived on Rue Dulac in the 15ème arrondissement of Paris—one half mile from Matisse's residence and studio in the former Convent Sacre-Coeur on the corner of Rue du Invalides and Rue Babylone. Matisse had just moved there in 1907 and opened an art school in 1908 shortly before Moser arrived in Paris.[13] Moser studied at the Académie Colarossi, an art school that Matisse attended with fellow Fauves Albert Marquet and Jean Puy six years earlier.[14] Matisse maintained a relationship with the school, and as late as 1908 it was reported that: "[he] could be seen drawing near the door most afternoons enveloped in a black sheepskin coat, turned wool side out, with a square-cut red beard, strong features and large shining eyes—a sight you couldn't overlook—that was Henri Matisse."[15]

In the autumn of 1907 Matisse kept an "open house in his studio" where he would show his old work to visitors and answer their questions. Anyone could attend "but those who turned up seem to have been mostly foreign art students from Colarossi's."[16] "Germans, or Americans of German origin…"[17] were particularly well-represented; Moser, who was born in Switzerland and spoke German, would have felt most welcome in that company. Matisse's educational generosity would also have attracted someone in Moser's economic circumstances. As art historian and Matisse scholar Hilary Spurling has shown, "Word that tuition was free soon got round the foreign colonies of Montparnasse and numbers exploded. Students poured in that autumn (1908) from all over Europe and America…"[18] While no documentation has been discovered confirming Moser's attendance at Matisse's school, his close proximity to a tuition-free opportunity known to and frequented by students of the Academie Colarossi makes a compelling circumstantial case.[19]

Yet, even if Moser did not attend Matisse's school, or never met Matisse or any of the other Fauves, he would have been exposed to their work as Fauvism remained a subject of controversy in 1908. The Sixth Salon d'Automne at the Grand Palais ended in November, the last time the original Fauves would exhibit together. Matisse alone exhibited 11 paintings, 6 drawings and several sculptures, though Camoin, Derain, Flandrin, Friesz, Manguin, Marquet, Marval, Puy, Valtat, and Vlaminck all participated.[20] In addition. Fauvism was national news the very month Moser arrived as Matisse had just returned from Berlin where he had attempted to install his works at the Paul Cassirer Gallery. Negative advance criticism in the German press prompted Cassirer to refuse some of Matisse's paintings. The Lepzig Kunstchronik's critic commented, "I stand speechless in front of these extravaganzas and, I confess it openly, have only one feeling in response to them: a huge, irrepressible impulse to laugh!" The publicity surrounding this German rebuke made Matisse something of a hero when he returned to Paris.[21]

While Fauvism proper was winding down just before Moser's arrival in France, during his tenure in Paris, Fauvist works were constantly on exhibit in close proximity to Moser's activities.[22] These exhibits were free to the public and were usually accompanied by a printed catalog and press reviews that often generated negative publicity about this controversial new art movement. While the specific details of Moser's exposure to the Fauves and their works may be lost to history, it is clear that when he returned home he was influenced by the compelling force of Fauvism.

Moser completed his training in Paris and returned to the United States in July 1910. Returning to Utah, Moser eventually turned his back on the academic training he received in Paris and evolved his own distinctive style. Initially, Henri experienced considerable success as an artist. In 1914 he was awarded the *Utah Art Prize* by the Utah State Institute of Fine Arts for his 1913 painting *After the Storm*. In 1915 he received first prize at the Utah State Fair for *Edwin Bridge* which was purchased by the State and displayed in the Capitol building. *The Poplars* was awarded the Purchase Prize at the

1926 State Fair and was the third and last painting procured by the State.[23] It was during this time, however, that Moser discovered his mature style, as he began using a freer palette and looser concept of form inspired by the Fauvist influences from his days in Paris.

In the same way that the French Fauves, through direct experience of location, audaciously transposed the scenery of Collioure, London, Saint Tropez, L'Estaque, La Seine and Antwerp, Moser painted Bear Lake, the Tetons, Southern Utah, Logan Canyon and other western landscapes into incandescent scenes of another world. His response to nature was direct and emotional and his paintings instill a sense of joy and well being. The Fauves separated color from its descriptive, representational purpose and allowed it to exist on the canvas as an independent element; Moser painted turquoise mountains, magenta skies, pink trees, orange hills and purple lakes, using saturated colors directly from the tube. The Fauves also believed that details in a painting disturbed its emotional value; hence, they chose bold, broken, and unmodified brush work to make the painting spontaneous and emotional. Moser's brushwork is impetuous, it vibrates with energy and emotion, bordering on the chaotic. Still, "the visual disturbance is only transitory. Somehow all the elements seem to fall back into place."[24] Neo-Impressionist like brushstrokes of pure color are seen in Moser's *Redstone Canyon* (1929), with unpainted areas of the canvas showing through between the turquoise, green and purple blocks of paint. The foreground of *Sardine Canyon* (1924) reveals a van Gogh-like impasto as Moser plays with thickly textured brushstrokes.

But, Moser was not merely a Fauve imitator; his style and approach to painting is distinctive and unique. As Utah scholar and art historian James Hazeltine opined, "In the final analysis what keeps an artist's work alive is a personal point of view. He must forget about playing it safe, staying with a sure formula."[25] I believe Moser's best works are those that use fully saturated colors to create a sense of space, as he expresses the structure, form and essence of the landscape not through linear perspective but through emotional color. *Red Butte River* (no date), *Tetons from Jenny's Lake* (1930), *Murray Canyon from Wellsville Dam* (1931) and *Pink Mountain* (no date) are examples of Moser's unique interpretation of the Cezanne influenced Fauvism of 1907–08. Here Moser used color with abandon to explore the Cezanne-like creation of space, form and structure. As art historian James Haseltine observed Henri Moser's "incandescent canvases of canyons, mountains, lakes and flowers are of another world. The Persian concept of the garden as paradise is expanded to include the whole of creation. In Moser's garden of delights it is always summer, always high noon. All shapes are positive, all hues at full saturation."[26]

Moser had revealed his true self, and had finally achieved his goal of using art to express the joy he felt experiencing the natural world. However, "painting with his heart" did not generate the living that Henri needed to support his family of eight children. This meant that a series of jobs occupied much of the time that he would have wished to be painting. Initially he taught at the Utah Agricultural College (Now Utah State University) to fulfill his commitment to Dr. Widtsoe. From 1915 to 1917 he accepted another teaching position at the Branch Agricultural College in Cedar City where he painted *Edwin Bridge*. From 1917 to 1925 Moser homesteaded and later purchased a ranch near Malad. In 1929, he accepted the position of Art Supervisor for the Cache Valley School district, for which he travelled from school to school offering art demonstrations and instructions for generations of children. On September 1, 1951 at age 76, he succumbed to pneumonia.[27] His final work, painted less than a month before his passing reflects the same incandescent color that so powerfully influenced him in Paris.[28] Although his bold use of color and unique style had often shocked an aesthetically conservative public accustomed to the naturalistic work of earlier Utah artists, Moser had pressed forward with conviction. He "stayed with the grand tradition of the ages in that an artist should paint with his own heart, as he sees and feels."[29]

MOSER'S PLACE IN ART HISTORY

As Apostle Widtsoe observed, Henri Moser "had to battle for his rights and place among those who give gifts to the world." Moser was a founding member of the Logan Artists Group that was organized in 1943 to "unify the efforts of professional artists…to avoid misconceptions concerning art on the part of the public."[30] The Group was organized in response to efforts by the conservative Utah art establishment to oppose the exhibition and promotion of "modern art in Utah." According to the organizational minutes, several Utah artists including, Avard Fairbanks, Dean of the Fine Arts Department at the University of Utah and a respected sculptor of Church history, "were against progressive art in Utah and did as much as they could to hinder the movement."[31] Despite that opposition, Henri found a market for his "progressive" paintings and according to a biographical reference in the Logan Artist Group papers "sold as many paintings as any painter in the state" including sales to "Universities and public schools in Utah and Idaho.[32] Moser's works continue to be popular in Utah, becoming "more and more sought after as the years go on."

Mosers "legacy," however, remains primarily a local one. William H. Gerdts, described Moser as a "pioneer in Expressionism and a pivotal influence on the local art scene." Utah art historian James L. Haseltine referred to Moser as "Utah's Fauve" and "one of only three artists who might be called expressionists." Robert S. Olpin also recognized Moser's contributions to modernism. Studies on expressionism or fauvism in America, however, neglect to recognize Henri Moser or his role as an early pioneer in American Expressionism.[33]

Great artists are often not appreciated until long after their time. Revolutionary styles, by definition, cut against conventional wisdom: Haseltine remarked upon Moser's revolutionary qualities, writing:

> "At first viewing [Moser's paintings] are to many people painful pictures. Some appear to
> be simply vignettes: trees sometimes march in awkward columns across the canvas, viridian
> lakes gash the landscape, magenta cliffs wound the mountains. Yet, the visual disturbance is
> only transitory. Somehow all the elements seem to fall back into place. Through the artist's

integrity, consistency and passion of his vision, and his orchestration of color, we are finally convinced that these paintings work. The intense, unexpurgated, often naive, art of Henri Moser demands a sophisticated viewer." [34]

Sophistication, however, is not required to appreciate what I believe to be Moser's greatest gift: an art that sustains the spirit and provides momentary refuge from the adversities of life; a revitalizing experience that helps us face life's demands and bear its disappointments with greater resilience and hope. As his wife Aldine wrote years after his death, "as I look upon the lovely pictures on my walls, I feel that his spirit is still here with me and I feel refreshed from my labors." [35] Aldine's words mirror those of another great artist named Henri, who said that art should have "a soothing, calming influence on the mind, something like a good armchair which provides relaxation from physical fatigue." [36]

In terms of artistic theory, Moser, like Matisse, was less concerned with the nature of images, or as art historian Remi Labrusse explained, "their figurative or abstract relation to external reality, but more with their action in stimulating a response in those who came across them." [37] Matisse "was intuitively seeking to redefine artistic creation not as a matter of ontology (the essence of forms) but of phenomenology (their effect): what obsessed him was the dynamics of our relationship to images, rather than the images themselves." [38]

In the less technical words of the devoutly religious Logan painter who, at the urging of Latter Day Saint Apostle John A. Widstoe, traveled to Paris in 1908 to study art just as Matisse was concluding his revolutionary Fauvist period, artistic creation "is a special gift from God to Man." [39] Moser used that gift to stimulate a joyous spiritual response in those who make an effort to appreciate and experience his vision. Those privileged to at least glimpse that world through Henri's art understand that aesthetic perception can be a sublime way of discovering truth; a truth experience more profound than the power of any words to express.

Mark Callister graduated from the University of Utah College of Law in 1984 and is the co-author of several legal publications. After retiring from the practice of law in 2014, he graduated from the Weber State University Law Enforcement Academy and served as a patrol deputy with the Davis County Sheriff and an instructor at the Academy. As an avid art collector and researcher with interests in Henri Moser, Maynard Dixon and the French Fauves (among others) he serves as a member of the Acquisition Committee for the State of Utah Alice Merrill Horne Art Collection. Mark and his wife Susan have four children, four grandchildren, and live in Farmington Utah.

End Notes

1. John A. Widtsoe, Personal Letter to Aldine Moser, 3 September 1951, quoted in Thomas Moyle Alder, *Pathway to Color: The Art and Life of Henri Moser*, Masters Thesis, University of Utah 2007. Tom Alder was a prominent Utah art dealer and the leading authority on Henri Moser. The author is much indebted to Tom for his gracious guidance and expertise in preserving the legacy of this great artist.

2. See generally, Russell T. Clement, *Les Fauves A Sourcebook* (Connecticut: Greenwood Press, 1994); Jean Paul Crespelle, *The Fauves* (Connecticut: The New York Graphic Society, 1962), pp. 49–56; John Elderfield, *"The Wild Beasts" Fauvism and its Affinities* (New York: The Museum of Modern Art, Oxford University Press, 1976), pp. 13–18.

3. For this excellent summary of fauvism see Justin Wolf, The Art Story Foundation, Fauvism, https://m.theartstory.org/movement/fauvism/.

4. Alder, .26-27.

5. The Académie Colarossi was an art school in Paris founded in the 19th century by the Italian sculptor Filippo Colarossi. First located on the Île de la Cité, it moved in the 1870s to 10 rue de la Grande-Chaumière in the 6th arrondissement. The school attracted many foreign students, including a large number from the United States.

6. The Académie Delécluse was an atelier-style art school in Paris, France, founded in the late 19th century by the painter Auguste Joseph Delécluse. It was exceptionally supportive of women artists, with more space being given to women students than men. It was located in Montparnasse on the Rue Notre Dame des Champs.

7. Alder, 35. Jean Paul Laurens (1838–1921) was a French painter and sculptor, and one of the last major exponents of the French Academic style. Strongly anti-clerical and republican, his work was often on historical and religious themes, through which he sought to convey a message of opposition to monarchical and clerical oppression. His erudition and technical mastery were much admired in his time, but in later years his highly realistic technique came to be regarded by some art-historians as overly didactic. https://en.wikipedia.org/wiki/Jean-Paul_Laurens. Lucien Simon was a French painter who taught at the Académie Colarossi and the École Nationale des Beaux-Arts. In 1937 he won First Prize at "l'Exposition universelle de Paris" for his work on the Luxembourg pavilion.

8. See Emily C. Burns, "Of a Kind Hitherto Unknown": *The American Art Association of Paris in 1908, Journal of Nineteenth Century Art Worldwide*, Volume 14, Issue 1 (Spring 1915).

9. *Alder*, 30 citing a February 21, 1909 Letter to Aldine.

10. *Alder*, 29–30

11. *Alder*, 39, citing November 14 1909 letter to Aldine.

12. Robert S. Olpin, William C. Seifrit, Vera G. Swanson, *Artists of Utah* (Layton: GibbsSmith Publisher, 1999), 293.

13. Hilary Spurling, *The Unknown Matisse* (New York: Alfred Knopf), 407.

14. Ibid, 197, 200.

15. Ibid, 402.

16. Ibid, 405.

17. Ibid, 410.

18. Spurling, 12–13.

19. Olpin, Seifrit, and Swanson include a quote from Moser, stating: "I knew Picasso in Paris in 1910. He painted beautiful things then. Today he paints to advertise himself, laughs at the credulous public. But he has great ability." Tom Alder identified the source as an article published in the Salt Lake Tribune, 18 July 1948 by reporter Grace Grether, who had interviewed Moser for a Pioneer Day celebration. See Alder, 110.

20. See, *The Fauve Landscape* (Los Angeles County Museum of Art 1990), 112.

21. *The Fauve Landscape*, 115.

22. An incomplete list of such exhibitions includes the following: Galerie Berthe Weill exhibited paintings by Manguin, Marquet, Matisse and Puy from December 11–31, 1908. The Galerie Notre-Dame-des-Champs exhibited three paintings by Braque, three by Derain, four by Dufy and two by Picasso from December 21 to January 15, 1909. Galerie Druet exhibited paintings by Flandrin, Friesz, Laprade, Manguin, Marquet, Marval, Puy, Van Dongen from December 31 to January 16, 1909. Galerie Eugene Blot exhibited works by Flandrin, Laprade, Matisse, Manguin, Marquet and Puy from November 13 through December 4, 1909. Ambroise Vollard hosted an exposition for Jean Puy at his gallery from November 30 through December 30, 1908. Ambroise Vollard exhibited 50 works by Louis Valtat at his gallery through March 18,1909. Galerie Druet exhibited works by Van Dongen, Matisse, Puy, Flandrin, Laprade and Marval from December 1909 through January 1910. Galerie Devambez exhibited paintings by Flandrin, Laprade, Manguin and Marquet from January18 2009 to February 5, 2010. Vollard exhibited 37 paintings and ceramics by Maurice de Vlaminck at his gallery from March 15th through the 26th in 1910.

23. Alder, *35–40*.

24. James L. Haseltine, *100 years of Utah Painting*, (Salt Lake City: Salt Lake Art Center, 1965), 36.

25. Ibid. According to Haseltine, after 100 years of Utah art, there are only six artists who meet this standard—"Evans, Mahonri Young, Beauregard, Stewart, Moser and Larsen."

26. Haseltine, 36.

27. Alder, 105–108.

28. See Alder, Figure 25, Laguna, CA, dated 1951; numbered 1,198. Moser family, collection. Figure 25. Henri Moser, Final painting of Laguna, CA, dated 1951 ; numbered 1, 198.

29. Robert, S. Olpin, *Dictionary of Utah Art*, The Salt Lake Art Center, 1980 at p. 166.

30. See, Constitution Of the Logan Artists Group, Article II, Section 1, Utah State University Special Collections Mss.126, Box 1, Folder 1. Calvin Fletcher, Dean of the Utah State Art Department, was also a founding member and is credited with introducing Utah to "modern art."

31. Ibid.

32. Ibid. According to the Group notes "up to 1948, [Moser} had sold 1013 paintings."

33. See *Introduction to Fauvism*, Teta Collins and Lonnie Dunbier, http://www.askart.com/art/Styles/47/y/Fauves-Fauvism, 2018.

34. *Haseltine,2.*

35. Aldine Moser, unpublished Autobiography, 1958.

36. "What I dream of is an art of balance, of purity and serenity, devoid of troubling or depressing subject matter, an art which could be for every mental worker, for the businessman as well as the man of letters, for example, a soothing, calming influence on the mind, something like a good armchair which provides relaxation from physical fatigue." Henri Matisse, 'Notes d'un Peintre' (Notes of a Painter) *La Grande Revue*, (Paris, 25 December 1908).

37. Remi Labrusse, *Fauvism a Word and A Thing in Matisse and the Fauves* (Vienna: Weinland Verlag, 2013), pp. 257-60.

38. Ibid.

39 Alder, 22, citing a June 10, 1909 letter to Aldine

Henri Moser: Recollections of a Grandaughter and Collector

Sharron Brim is the granddaughter of John Henri Moser, and many of the paintings in this exhibition are from her collection. In a recorded interview on February 12, 2020 she gave the following brief account of her memories of her grandfather:

My grandfather, John Henri Moser, married Aldine Wursten in 1905. They had eight children, two boys and then six daughters. My mother Louise was the second oldest daughter. She had two daughters, my sister Maurine and then me.

Henri and my grandmother Aldine lived in Logan in a big White House on Fourth North. Grandpa's art studio in the back of the property.. I went to live with them when I was seven because my parents separated. My father joined the Navy and my mother moved to Salt Lake to try to get a better salary and learn a profession. Maurine and I stayed with our grandparents for four years.

I was born in California and we made visits back to Logan, but I didn't really know my grandparents well until we moved back to Utah after the attack on Pearl Harbor in 1941. We lived in the house next door. At that time, Grandma Aldine was cooking meals for a fraternity house and she had four boarders in the room that later became our bedroom. Grandma was always doing something to earn a little living because Grandpa's income wasn't always steady.

When my parents separated and I went to live with my grandparents in 1943, my Grandpa Henri had been home for a year after an eleven month long stay in the hospital following his terrible accident

Opposite:
Quaking Aspens Old Homestead
1930, oil on board,
24 x 20 inches
Sharron Brim Collection, detail.

in 1941. This accident occurred when he was employed as the art supervisor for the Cache County School district. He was driving to River Heights in his Model-T in February, the roads were icy, and his car skidded off what is known as the Dugway in the Logan River Heights area. The ambulance came and they took him to the hospital with punctured lungs, broken ribs and a shattered hip. The doctors didn't know if he was going to make it but he's a fighter and he was strong. They put his hip back together with plates and screws and he ended up with one of his legs shortened by two to three inches. His foot was always swollen and was about three times the size of the other foot. His friend Bernie Berenson was a violin maker in town, and he designed this special shoe that Grandpa had to wear with a $2\frac{1}{2}$ to 3" thick sole that enabled him to walk without a limp.

While Grandpa was in the hospital, he had colored pencils that he used to make beautiful pictures. I have two of those pictures hanging in my home. He would lick the pencils to make it look like paint or watercolor, and he would give these pictures away to people in the hospital. Grandpa was a positive, cheerful person. That is how he got over his accident because he was so positive.

Grandpa was a big man. He was six feet one or two inches. He was very patriotic, loved his country and wanted to do his part in the war effort. Grandpa joined the Pipefitters union in Portland, Oregon, and they gave him a job scraping rust from old ship parts so that they could use them to build the new ships. While hitchhiking to Portland with a stiff leg and cane, a gentleman in a black limousine picked him up and took Grandpa the entire way from Logan to Oregon. When they arrived in Portland Grandpa introduced this man to his daughters Ruth and Maurine who lived in Portland. The man said, "I just want to tell you, ladies, that this is the most fascinating man I've ever met in my life. This has been the most enjoyable, wonderful trip I've ever taken. His conversation and stories and reciting of poetry just kept me mesmerized the entire trip. You are really lucky to have this man for your father." I love that story.

While he was in Oregon my dear grandmother took care of us. She is an angel. Previously, my sister and I had had kind of an erratic, disruptive childhood and had moved around a lot. So, I found myself in this nice stable home with a loving grandmother and grandpa that I loved and respected. They provided the stability for me that I wouldn't have otherwise had. My grandmother taught me the gospel and instilled my love for God and the Savior. I will never stop being grateful to her for that. When I turned eight, she took me to be baptized in the Logan temple. From that time on I spent many, many Saturdays walking to the temple by myself to do baptisms for the dead, because my great grandmother and my great aunt had done all this temple work and my sister and I and one other cousin were delegated to be the ones baptized for our ancestors. I loved it. I just cherish those times because I love the temple. My grandmother Aldine went regularly to the temple.

My grandfather impressed me as an imposing man when he walked into the room. You noticed because he was tall and slender and stood as straight as an arrow, even with his poor leg, straight as an arrow. He had all that white hair and dimples in each cheek and a big dimple in his chin. He wasn't a loquacious person but when he talked, you listened. He had a wonderful speaking voice, low and warm and kind of dramatic. He told stories or experiences with flair, I mean, you were taken in and there was a slight air of drama, but that's how he felt about it and he made you feel it too. Grandpa was tolerant, never judgmental. He was a very learned man and very well read. His vocabulary was impressive. He knew all the classics, he could quote Shakespeare, he knew poetry. He knew every poem in his favorite anthology book and could recite it to you. It was just a joy to him. He also wrote poetry.

One of his favorite friends was Professor Potts from the university. He would come and they would talk about art and philosophy. I remember they talked about Nietzsche. That was the level of conversation that Grandpa enjoyed. He read the paper from front to back and listened to the news. He had a broad range of friends, from the professors at the college, other artists and art dealers like Alice Merrill Horne and common folks. To every person he would meet, he tipped his hat and he said something warm and wonderful. He loved people and he was interested in them. Most people at church and in town called him Professor Moser.

One day he had gone to town and Grandma had this urgent errand that I had to run for her. I think I had to go to J.C. Penney's and get her something immediately, so I ran downtown past the tabernacle, and I looked over at the courthouse and there was Grandpa. They had big benches out in front of the courthouse and everybody from every walk of life came there to sit and talk with each other and visit. I didn't know Grandpa did that, but it was a way for him to rest before walking back home. I saw him from across the street. All his friends gathered around him and they were talking, and he was leaning on his cane. He was comfortable in that setting. There were people in overalls and of all different ethnicities just listening to Grandpa. And then he would listen to them. I just stood there and took that in. I thought—this is my grandpa, he's comfortable anywhere.

Grandpa was unflappable. I remember when he and some other artists, Calvin Fletcher, Esther Poulson, and one other had been out painting together and they returned to the house. I wanted to see them, and I wanted to hear what they were going to do, so I was peeking around the stairwell, and I could see through the baluster they brought in an easel, and they wanted to look at each other's work for the day. I don't know who went first, but I remember when Grandpa put his painting on the easel and Dr. Fletcher came around and looked at it, I was waiting to see everybody's reaction. Dr. Fletcher said something like "John that isn't what we saw today! You added things in there in all that unrealistic color." I am sitting there, incensed that someone is criticizing my grandfather. The other artists were looking at it, too. Then Grandpa said in his very calm, dignified and grand way, "Well, I painted what I saw." His chin was up, and he was proud of what he did. There was just silence in the room. Just silence. That is how Grandpa was. He never argued with people. He politely, kindly, and genteelly stated his opinion. I loved that about him. I think he taught me to stand up for myself and trust my own opinion.

I do not know much about Henri's childhood, only what I've read in his short autobiography or heard from my grandparents or my mother. I assume that Henri and his mother heard the message of the gospel through missionaries in Switzerland. I think his mother and father divorced. His mother, Henri and other siblings emigrated from Switzerland. He was baptized after he arrived in America. From age 12 to 20 he lived with the Diem family in Payson, who were Swiss immigrants. He loved them dearly.

He worked hard to earn money for college. Grandpa was brilliant and apparently quite good at math. He went to the Utah State Agricultural College in Logan and registered as an engineering student. When his professors, especially Professor Stoddard, saw Grandpa's work, they said, "John, you need to be an artist." Grandpa loved art and drawing. He enrolled in some art classes taught by A. B. Wright that qualified him for study in Paris. Elder John A. Widstoe, who at that time was president of the college, recognized Grandpa's artistic ability. Elder Widstoe signed for the bank loan that enabled Grandpa to have the money to go to Paris on the condition that he would teach at the college after he returned.

About two years before Paris, Grandpa met my grandmother. He had gone to a grocery store, and he saw this beautiful girl working there. I'm sure he couldn't get her out of his mind because after a short time he came back to the store and gave her a letter that contained his proposal. He knew he was going to marry that woman. She told him "you are too late; I am engaged to someone else". That didn't deter him in any way, shape or form because he knew he wanted to marry her. He was relentless; and she was swept off her feet by this tall, handsome, determined young man.

They were married in Logan and had two little boys, a toddler and a baby, when Grandpa announced that he needed to go to Paris. They had just bought a little two room house on Tenth North up by the college. Grandma knew it was for the better good and could see the big picture. She knew that Henri believed he was called by God to be an artist and that he had to take advantage of this great opportunity. So, he left this beautiful young wife with these two babies and little means of support. Grandma told me that she had a beautiful garden and fruit trees that she worked to provide food for the family. She took in laundry and ironing so that she didn't have to leave the boys. She rented out the living room to a student couple that had babies of their own. She worked very hard, but she was happy. Grandma was always positive and faithful. She knew that God would bring her through. Her mother and her brothers and sisters all lived close by, so she had a support system. She and her family immigrated from Switzerland when she was eight years old.

I love to read the letters that they wrote back and forth when Henri was in Paris. My grandmother always talked in her letters about church and the gospel, and she sent him church books. He was a good-looking man in Paris all by himself without a family but I'm sure that his belief kept him true and faithful to her. I just feel that strongly. He was in a little one room that he rented with a little stove and he cooked for himself because he did not have any money. He lived for grandmother's letters. He enrolled in several art schools and he joined the American Art Association in Paris. I wish his letters included more information about art, but he always thought of himself as the only artist in the family and he kind of lived in his separate world. I don't think he shared a lot of details with Grandma about things having to do with his art, though she was a brilliant woman and would have probably enjoyed knowing more.

Grandpa had a love affair with nature. He knew every crevice, every color, everything about Bear Lake, the Grand Tetons, and Logan and Sardine Canyons. We often drove up Logan Canyon, and he usually sat in the back seat because of his straight stiff leg. I could hear him sighing and gasping to himself saying things like, "this is so dramatic." He saw the depth of every pigment and color that few people, I think, ever see. Every view was beautiful to him. He was so enchanted by it. He didn't talk to us in the car. He was by himself like someone living in another world seeing these views for the first time. In a letter to his wife he said' "I and nature have formed a partnership. She loves me because I am beginning to know her. She speaks to me each day as I meet her and sings her little songs to me as I wander through the woods or in the fields. She is my only company…. Now I must tell you that the season has come on when nature sings to me the most…. I enjoy the sunset, the afterglow of its rich effects. I love to watch the purple clouds send their colored tints on the fading leaves…. Fall has come on and every piece of nature is ripening with rich color. The foliage is all the richest colors and the skies or heavens are full with soft fleecy clouds like I have never in my life seen before."

I would often watch him paint in his studio, that wonderful studio. He built the studio before his accident. I remember coming back to Logan from California on a trip and my dad, who was an expert carpenter, helped Henri and another son in law build a 2-1/2 car garage with a second story art studio. On the south side there was a bay window and the whole north side was also windows. There was a big oak roll top desk with all his books and his writing paper. He had a stove and a heater, so it was always warm. He painted down on the west end of the studio. His easel was always up, and he had a big, long table, which he painted a bright aqua blue, where he kept all his brushes, palettes, and an open painter's box full of tubes of paint and brushes. Grandma made him a beautiful woven rag rug out of all bright colored fabric. She also made a coverlet for his single bed. He collected beautiful fabrics. I mean, I'm reminded of that Matisse painting where this woman is dressed in colorful pieces of fabric that he also used in the backgrounds of his paintings. Grandma made him a hat with these fabrics which he would wear to town. Grandma was a wonderful seamstress.

It was also my job to take his lunch up to him in the studio. I would go up there and open the door so quietly. I would come in and put his soup down on his big desk. Sometimes I would say, "Hi Grandpa."

Usually he would not say anything and would answer me with this funny little squeak noise he made with his mouth. His concentration was so deep. You did not talk when you went into his studio, and he was painting. You knew not to talk. Sometimes it seemed like hours before he would put on another stroke. I watched as he stood with a brush in his hand looking at the painting for long periods, just thinking about the next brush stroke. I would go lie down on that big rug in that warm, beautiful, spacious room with the smell of his paints and his linseed oil and turpentine. I mean, I just loved all of it. I would lie down on that rug and sometimes I would take drawing paper to draw or to read, but I just enjoyed being there with my grandpa. He was the male figure in my childhood because my dad was gone. I treasure those moments. I just remember how good I felt when I was up there, and I was just watching him paint.

When it came to selling his paintings, Grandpa was not very organized. Grandpa did not keep good records and he did not always follow through. He did not keep a ledger like he should have. When he died there were paintings all over town that had not been paid for. Grandma's efforts to collect were not successful. Henri's children's doctor's appointments, dental appointments, and music instruments were all paid for with paintings. Grandma and Grandpa's house was filled with this beautiful Stickley furniture that belonged to President Chase of the college. Grandpa traded several large paintings for the furniture. A beautiful dining room table and eight chairs, a gorgeous upright piano with candelabra, and a large library table that everyone would use to study. I mean, it was beautiful. They had a Stickley flower stand that stood in front of the front window with a big green fern flowing from it. Grandpa acquired all these things with his paintings.

In 1929, Grandpa started working as the art supervisor for the Cache county school district, a job he held for 21 years. He drove around to the different schools and gave art lessons. He contributed a lot of paintings to the Cache County schools. Before we moved in with Grandpa we were visiting from California, I must have been just four or five. I remember looking out of the north bedroom window and there was Grandpa in the back with a whole group of art students and there were these big tubs of mud sitting on the ground. I realized that it was clay. He had taken an art class up the canyon and had taught them how to find clay and dig it up themselves. He taught them how to work it and sculpt with it.

Whenever Grandpa saw a beautiful rock on one of his painting trips or excursions in the Canyon, he couldn't help himself. He put it in the back of his Model-T and brought it home. Now, we can't do that today, but Grandpa did that wherever he went until he had accumulated a lot of these beautiful stones. Rocks with sparkly things, rust veins and wonderful colors running through the surface. He used these beautiful rocks to face the south side of his studio, and to line the garden, the flower beds around the house, and the driveway. There used to be a median running up the middle of fourth north that was bordered with Grandpa's beautiful rocks and flowers.

He also beautified the world by planting flowers. He planted hollyhocks, sunflowers and beautiful blue flowers. He put hollyhocks all along his driveway. He gathered the seeds and taught us how to gather big bags of seeds that he would take on his trips and plant along the side of the road. He planted them along the roads of Sardine Canyon, and you can still see hollyhocks by the old canyon road. He planted flowers in Logan Canyon. He planted those seeds everywhere. He wanted to beautify the earth because he loved color.

Grandpa had many friends that would come by to visit with him in the studio. I remember a visit from Alice Merrill Horne who was Grandpa's art dealer and someone who championed Henri's work. I could tell that she had this amazing respect and love for Grandma and Grandpa. I didn't know this at the time because it happened before I came on the scene, but Grandma had a thyroid condition and had to have surgery. Alice's son was a doctor and so she had Grandma go to Salt Lake to have the surgery done by her son and another doctor. Grandma convalesced for weeks in Alice's home. Alice gave a reception for Grandma and Grandpa and invited many artists and important people like Heber J. Grant.

Being married to an artist was not easy. Grandpa decided to homestead a ranch in Daniels, Idaho in 1920. People told Grandma, "don't do it. Don't go up there. Don't do it, because he's going to leave you there and go off and paint." And he did. So, during the winter, he would leave on painting trips. He went to Texas. He went to San Francisco. He would go back to Logan leaving Aldine with the two boys and young girls. His two sons didn't like ranch or farm work and thought Grandpa was a little harsh on them. They were incredible musicians. Uncle Marcel played the trombone. He could make you weep; it was so beautiful. And Uncle Truman played the trumpet. They never had lessons. They left for California because they had had it with the ranch. Grandma kind of understood and supported them. When they left the six younger girls had to help Grandma run the ranch in the winter because Grandpa was always gone. They moved to the ranch when my mother was about seven and they came back when she was about fourteen. Mother and my aunts did men's work when they were like ten and eleven. When my mother was twelve, she drove a team of horses. They did the plowing and they worked like men. Daniels Idaho was a remote forsaken place. Life was hard there.

The Moser family loved music. Henri had a good singing voice, and sometimes I would hear him singing in the bathroom. He played the fiddle. Don't ask me where it came from, but he could fiddle. In Daniels, Idaho, he played and sang at Church parties and other social gatherings; he sang with my mother, and they made up songs and lyrics. "Mrs. Gruber's Boarding House" was one of their songs; it had six verses that Grandpa made up. They just had this little routine to entertain people. Grandpa and my mother sang and yodeled together.

When they first moved to Idaho the church called Henri to be Sunday School superintendent. They did not have an organist, so they called my grandmother to be the organist. Grandma was a singer, but she never had piano lessons or any music training. She said, "no, I can't" but they called her anyway. Somehow, she taught herself how to play. My grandmother could play every hymn in the hymnbook. She taught herself every hymn. These people were just smart, and they just could do things. They never expected life to be easy. They just took each challenge with grit and positivity and knew with their faith they could do it. Never once, did I hear them complain. That's how our family is. That's how I am. That's how my grandparents were. They taught us to be brave and courageous and face our trials and challenges.

My sister and I were home alone when the telegram came informing us of our father's death on Iwo Jima in 1945. He died in February, but we did not get the telegram until March 17th right before my birthday. When the telegram arrived, we were by ourselves playing in the little grass skirts and hula outfits that my father had woven and made for us while he was stationed in Hawaii before he shipped out to the Pacific front. Our mother was in Salt Lake working. We had to call her, and she was out to lunch or something. I remember my sister saying, would you just tell her that our daddy died? It was very hard. My grandparents were very stoic, but it really affected Grandpa because he loved my father. My father was a wonderful man and he had helped Grandpa build his studio. Grandpa took it very hard and he wrote a beautiful tribute to my dad that I cherish.

I think the car accident mellowed Grandpa. He was able to show his appreciation and gratitude and spend more time with his wife and family. When he would come in from the studio for breakfast and dinner Grandma was in the kitchen and he would take the lid off whatever she was cooking to see what she was making and smell it. I saw this every day. He would lean down and kiss the back of her neck and put his arm around her waist. He adored my grandmother. He loved her cooking; she was a spectacular cook. She had a hot breakfast every morning for us. We always had family prayer around this big oak table. It was always a kneeling prayer. Grandpa would get down on that poor leg and we would have family prayer in the morning. Then at night we would have dinner and he would come in from the studio and we would have family prayer and dinner. In the evenings, he would read the paper and he always wrote in his journal before returning to his studio.

Grandpa had a special relationship with my mother Louise, she was the "apple of his eye." They were very much alike. She loved to spend time with him. She didn't like housework. She wanted to be outside. Her sisters were all beautiful seamstresses and excellent homemakers. Now, my mother, no. She wanted to be out with Grandpa, and he loved having her by his side. Henri wasn't like other ranchers. He did not use the normal swear words that most farmers do with their animals. Mother said he would call them and say things like "get over here, you infernal reprobates." They slaughtered the pigs and she castrated cattle with him. She tended the milk cows and plowed. She did every-thing that the boys did, and they had a good time together; but it was hard, too.

In September 1951, after a long struggle with health problems relating to his accident, Grandpa developed pleurisy and pneumonia and was hospitalized. When Grandma sent the word that Grandpa was not expected to live, Mother was so concerned that she wouldn't make it in time. We left California immediately, and headed to Logan. She went straight up to the hospital and Dr. Paulson, Henri's dear friend and doctor, was crying and saying, "dear, dear John." Mother went to Grandpa's bedside. He had waited till she came. She was with him that night when he passed away. I am thankful for that. Mother loved her father's paintings and was Henri Moser's greatest advocate. She promoted and organized two exhibits of his work, one at Utah State and another in Salt Lake. It is because of her, and my own love for my grandparents, that I have felt a responsibility to promote my Grandfather's work and legacy.

Henri would be so happy with this exhibit and he would say, "good job, this is the best thing that could happen." I am sure he will be there. This reminds me of one last story. Our mother purchased her parents' house so when she passed away Maurine and I had to clean out decades of miscellaneous furniture, art supplies, paintings, and yard tools. Truckloads. I remember that we were out in the storage room underneath the studio, my sister was standing there with a big garbage bag and I was cleaning out some shelves and cabinets, just throwing old stuff away. I reached in and grabbed a wad of something, and I went to throw it in the garbage sack, but something prevented me, I felt very strongly that I needed to see what this was. I slowly unfolded the crumpled wad and saw that it was a canvas, a crumpled-up canvas. As I peeked in, I could see pink, then I could see yellow and then turquoise. I knew it was a painting that I needed to rescue and have restored. It was *The Pink Mountain*, the image on the poster promoting this exhibit.

Sharron Brim is the granddaughter of John Henri Moser and his wife Aldine. Having lived with her grandparents as a child, she has had a lifelong interest in her grandfather's work, and remains one of his most passionate and knowledgeable collectors. She and her husband Larry live in Provo, Utah, and maintain the website, http://henrimoser.org/ to share and promote Henri Moser's work.

Plate 1
A (Self-Portrait)
1910, oil on board, 31 x 25 ½ inches
Sharron Brim Collection

Plate 2
Untitled
1905, oil on board, 13 ¾ x 16 ¾ inches
Gift of Lyman Jensen. Collection of the Nora Eccles Harrison Museum of Art, Utah State University

Plate 3
French Landscape Near Paris
1909, oil on canvas, 17 ¾ x 31 ⅜ inches
Brigham Young University Museum of Art, 1935

Plate 4
Countryside Paris
1910, oil on board, 10 x 14 inches
Sharron Brim Collection

Plate 5
After the Storm
1913, oil on canvas, 21 x 36 inches
Utah Division of Arts and Museum Fine Arts Collection

Plate 6
Through the Trees
No date, oil on canvas, 30 ¼ x 16 inches
Utah Division of Arts and Museum Fine Arts Collection

Plate 7
Peaceful Evening
1915, oil on board, 8 x 17 inches
Susan and Mark Callister Collection

Plate 8
Pioneer Wagon Train
1917, oil, 36 x 48 inches
Courtesy of Church History Museum

Plate 9
Zions Canyon
No date, oil on board, 16 x 13 inches
Sharron Brim Collection

Plate 10
Southern Utah Mountains by Cedar City
1917, oil on canvas, 19 x 23 inches
Susan and Mark Callister Collection

Plate 11
Red Butte River
No date, oil, 22 x 16 inches
Courtesy of Church History Museum

Plate 12
The Edwin Bridge
1917, oil on canvas, 58 ½ x 36 inches
Utah Division of Arts and Museum Fine Arts Collection

Plate 13
Red Canyon (Red Stone Canyon, Zion)
Ca. 1920, oil on board, 35 ½ x 17 ¼ inches
Sharron Brim Collection

Plate 14
Red Stone Canyon, Zions
1929, oil on board, 19 x 23 inches
Susan and Mark Callister Collection

Plate 15
Untitled
1920, oil on canvas, 17 ⅜ x 29 ¼ inches
Gift of Ida Mae S. Mckay. Collection of the Nora Eccles Harrison Museum of Art, Utah State University

Plate 16
Logan Canyon Golden Aspens
No date, oil on board, 24 x 18 inches
Sharron Brim Collection

Plate 17
Logan Canyon Towards Beaver Mountain
1930, oil on board, 29 x 39 inches
Susan and Mark Callister Collection

Plate 18
Murray Canyon from Wellsville Dam (Wellsville Mountain)
1930, oil on board, 19 x 23 inches
Susan and Mark Callister Collection

Plate 19
Logan Canyon, Near Beaver Dam
1926, oil on canvas, 25 ¼ x 32 ¼ inches
Courtesy of Springville Museum of Art

Plate 20
Bear Lake
No date, oil on board, 5 ½ x 8 ½ inches
Susan and Mark Callister Collection

Plate 21
Bear Lake in Springtime Apple Blossom Time
1946, oil on board, 18 ¾ x 23 ½ inches
Collection of the Nora Eccles Harrison Museum of Art, Utah State University

Plate 22
Bear Lake
1931, oil on board, 8 x 6 inches
Susan and Mark Callister Collection

Plate: 23
Bear Lake with Orange Trees
No date, oil on Masonite, 28 x 24 inches
Sharron Brim Collection

Plate 24
Bear Lake Near Garden City
1926, oil on canvas board, 12 x 15 inches
Brigham Young University Museum of Art, gift of the family of Dr. and Mrs. Burtis France Robbins, 1962

Plate 25
Bear Lake South from Garden City
1929, oil on board, 11 ½ x 15 inches
Susan and Mark Callister Collection

Plate 26
White Pine Lake Above Tony's Grove
Ca. 1918, oil on board, 14 x 21 inches
Susan and Mark Callister Collection

Plate 27
Bear Lake with Clouds
Ca. 1930, oil on canvas board, 11 ½ x 17 inches
Susan and Mark Callister Collection

Plate 28
Pink Mountain
No date, oil on canvas board, 17 x 21 ½ inches
Sharron Brim Collection

Plate 29
Tall Golden Aspens (Golden Quaking Aspens)
No date, oil on board, 32 x 20 inches
Sharron Brim Collection

Plate 30
Tetons from Jenny Lake
1930, oil on board, 12 ½ x 15 ½ inches
Susan and Mark Callister Collection

Plate 31
Spring Mountain Scene
No date, oil on board, 20 x 23 inches
Susan and Mark Callister Collection

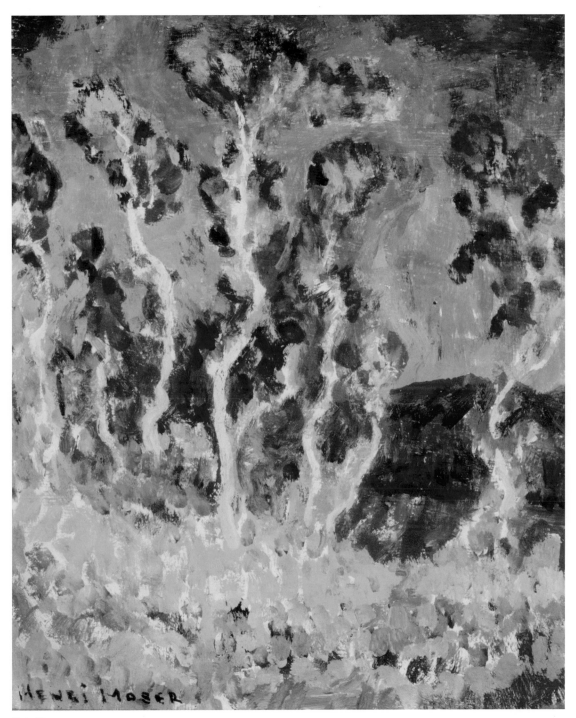

Plate 32
Green Aspens Blue Background
No date, oil on board, 12 x 10 inches
Sharron Brim Collection

Plate 33
Untitled
1920, oil on board, 22 x 18 ⅛ inches
Gift of Ida Mae S. Mckay. Collection of the Nora Eccles Harrison Museum of Art, Utah State University

Plate 34
Sardine Canyon
No date, oil on board, 19 x 23 inches
Susan and Mark Callister Collection

Plate 35
Orchard in Spring South of Wellsville
1926, oil on canvas, 19 $^7/_8$ x 28 inches
Courtesy of Springville Museum of Art

Plate 36
Goatherd
1929, oil on canvas board, 20 x 24 inches
Sharron Brim Collection

Plate 37
Blue Bonnets
1928, oil on board, 18 x 24 inches
Sharron Brim Collection

Plate 38
Quaking Aspens Old Homestead
1930, oil on board, 24 x 20 inches
Sharron Brim Collection

Plate 39
Moonlight Aspens (Golden Aspens in Moonlight)
No date, oil on canvas board, 24 x 20 inches
Sharron Brim Collection